THE OTHER SIDE

HOW THE TRUTH OF GRACE BRINGS
HEALING AND HOPE

JANET CARRUTHERS

The Other Side: How the Truth of Grace Brings Healing and Hope

© 2025 Janet Carruthers

All rights reserved.

No part of this publication may be reproduced, stored in a retrieval system, or transmitted in any form or by any means—electronic, mechanical, photocopying, recording, or otherwise—without prior written permission from the publisher, except for brief quotations used in reviews or articles.

Unless otherwise noted, all Scripture quotations are taken from the **World English Bible (WEB)**, a public domain translation.

This book is a work of nonfiction. Some names and identifying details may have been changed to protect privacy. Any similarity to persons living or deceased is purely coincidental.

ISBN: **979-8-89778-830-9**

Printed in the United States of America

First Edition

To my Lord -
The One who saw me, rescued me, and never let go.
I pray this book is worthy of the calling You placed on my heart. May every word point back to You. May every page reflect Your grace. Your Truth. The peace that only you can provide. And may even one soul find their way home through what You've written here.
This is for You.
Always.
Janet

CONTENTS

Acknowledgments	vii
Introduction	ix
1. Welcome to the Struggle	1
Reflection Questions	13
2. The Breaking Point	15
My Hope and Prayer for You	25
Reflection Questions	27
3. The God Who Never Left	29
My Hope and Prayer for You	37
Reflection Questions	39
4. Truth of Grace	41
My Hope and Prayer for You	47
Reflection Questions	49
5. The Long Road Forward	51
My Hope and Prayer for You	59
Reflection Questions	61
6. When Your View changes	63
My Hope and Prayer for You	69
Reflection Questions	71
7. Progress in the Mess	73
My Hope and Prayer for You	79
Reflection Questions	81
8. Finding Yourself Again	83
My Hope and Prayer for You	89
Reflection Questions	91
9. Hope Ahead	93
My Hope and Prayer for You	99
Reflection Questions	101
10. Keep Moving Forward	103
My Hope and Prayer for You	111
Reflection Questions	113
11. Invitation to Faith	115

ACKNOWLEDGMENTS

This book would not exist without the steady, unfailing grace of God. To my Heavenly Father—thank You for never leaving me, even when I doubted, wandered, or questioned.

To my parents in heaven—thank you for providing the legacy of the greatest peace of all: God. Your faith, your love, and your lives continue to echo through mine.

To my children, my greatest accomplishments—know that you are loved beyond words. You are my joy, my legacy, and my constant reminder of God's goodness.

To my husband, your support, patience, and love gave me the space to follow God's nudge and finally write what had been stirring in my heart for so long.

To my brothers, thank you for filling my life with laughter when I needed it most. I was always the serious one, the quiet one, and yes, the bossy one too—but you never let me stay too serious for long.

To my soul sisters—Gloria, Chinh, and Bette Jo—who believed in me in some of my darkest days. You stood by me when I couldn't see the way forward. Your love reminded me that I was never walking alone.

To my dearest friends and Connect Group who prayed for me, encouraged me, or believed in this message before it had a name, thank you. Your love fuelled the quiet, faithful work of writing.

To the readers: whether you're clinging to hope or rediscovering it, I wrote this for you. If even one person finds grace on the other side of pain because of these pages, then every early morning and every tear was worth it.

With love and gratitude,
    Janet Carruthers
    Truth of Grace Ministry

INTRODUCTION

There is always another side.

In this world, that truth is all around us. Every coin has one. Every story. Every heartbreak. Even the longest night eventually turns toward dawn.

And yet, when we're in the middle of struggle—grief, addiction, fear, shame, a physical illness, betrayal—it can feel like we're stuck in a one-sided reality.

Like this moment of pain is all there is.
　But what if there's more?
　What if the other side isn't just a possibility—it's a promise?

We don't always recognize it, but when we believe in God, we also believe in movement. In redemption. In restoration.

We believe that no matter how dark or heavy life becomes, God is already at work—waiting for us, calling us, gently guiding us to something deeper.

Something better.
　Something whole.

The other side isn't always instant.
Sometimes it's a long road.
Sometimes we crawl.

Sometimes we kick and scream the entire way… or maybe that's just me.

But this is true: God LOVES you and is always there.

On the other side of your brokenness.
    On the other side of your questions.
    On the other side of your anger.
    On the other side of the moment, you thought it might break you.

This book is an invitation. Not to skip the struggle.

But to walk through it with grace, with truth, and with God—until you discover what's been waiting for you all along:

    Healing.
    Hope.
    And Him.
    And here's what I've come to believe deep in my soul:
    It's the **truth of grace** that changes everything.

Grace isn't just a comforting idea—it's the powerful, unshakable truth that God meets us exactly where we are… not where we pretend to be.

Grace says:
    You're not too far gone.
    You're not too broken.
    You're not too late.

Grace is truth wrapped in love, and the thread runs through every page of this book.

And when we begin to see our lives through the lens of His grace, we start to see the other side, not as a distant hope, but as a present reality.

We don't always see it.

But the other side is always here.
And in case no one told you, **God loves you.**
…even if you're still on the other side.

CHAPTER 1
WELCOME TO THE STRUGGLE
EVERYONE IS WALKING THROUGH SOMETHING.

It started with traffic.

I was sitting in my car, crawling down the freeway at a pace that could only be described as glacial. I had just left work—late, exhausted, and cranky. It had been one of those days: too many meetings, not enough coffee, and more emails than any human should be expected to read. I was emotionally drained, physically tired, and mentally running on fumes.

And as I sat there gripping the steering wheel a little too tightly—thinking about the wet laundry I forgot to move to the dryer—a car in the next lane crept past me.

It had a bumper sticker that read: **"The struggle is real."**

And I laughed. Not a cute little giggle—one of those exhausted, borderline unhinged, crazy-lady laughs. Because in that moment, the bumper sticker was telling the absolute truth.

The struggle was real.
Traffic was real.
Work stress was real.

Life was real.

And I remember thinking, *"Why does everything feel so hard right now?"*

That moment didn't solve anything. I didn't suddenly get unstuck in traffic or magically feel better about my day. But it reminded me of something deeper: **we're all struggling in some way.** Sometimes it's small, like rush hour and a long to-do list. Other times, its heartbreak, illness, or loss.

The intensity changes, but the truth doesn't. **Struggle is part of the human experience.** And that's where this book begins.

If you're reading this, there's a good chance you're going through something—or maybe you just came out of something that shook you to your core. Either way, let me start by saying this clearly and gently:

You are not alone.

This book isn't going to offer you quick fixes or easy answers. Life rarely works that way. Instead, this is an invitation to walk with grace—at your own pace—through the things that have tried to break you. Through the questions, the pain, the silence, and even the anger.

Because the truth is, **struggle is part of every story.** It may look different for each of us, but none of us gets through life untouched by hardship.

Maybe your struggle has a name: grief, betrayal, depression, divorce, addiction, illness. Or maybe it doesn't.

Maybe it just feels like a heavy fog you can't explain to anyone else.
Whatever it is—

You're not weak.
You're not lost.
You're human.
And the struggle doesn't disqualify you from healing.
If anything, it's where healing begins.

WHEN LIFE BREAKS US

We all have a breaking point.

Sometimes it arrives suddenly, like a diagnosis or a disaster.

Other times it builds slowly, through unmet expectations, quiet disappointments, or years of holding everything together until something cracks.

It looks different for each of us, but it feels the same: A moment when something inside you whispers, *"I can't do this anymore."*

I once met a woman named Carla at a prayer retreat. She was kind and warm, but quiet, carrying something invisible.
During a small group session, she opened up. She had recently completed treatment for stage 4 cancer.
But her breaking point didn't happen in a hospital. It happened in the cereal aisle.

"I saw a box of my husband's favorite cereal," she said, "and I realized I wasn't sure I'd be here next month to buy it again."

That was the moment it all came crashing in.

I've had my own breaking point, too.
The day my father died of a sudden heart attack, the ground dropped out from under me.

We had just spoken. He had just turned 58.

He wasn't just my dad—he was my mentor, compass, and example of integrity and compassion. He reminded me to lead with kindness, stay grounded in my faith, and treat people the way Jesus would. And then, without warning, he was gone.

When someone that good, faithful, and impactful is taken so suddenly, it does more than shake your faith—it throws you into a storm you didn't see coming.

I sat there, numb and devastated, asking, *"Why, God? Why would You take someone like him?"*

He made a difference in every life he touched. He was one of the good ones.

And if I'm honest, I wasn't just heartbroken—I was angry.
Not at my father—but at God.

> At the loss.
> At the unfairness.
> At the silence.
> I didn't want comfort clichés or spiritual magic pills.
> I wanted answers.
> I wanted God to explain the reasoning.
> And yet—even in the ache—I kept showing up.

I journaled. I prayed. I paced. I sat in silence, sometimes just hoping God would say *something*.

It felt like I was in a deep hole, looking up at the light, unsure if I'd ever climb out. People tried to help. They showed up with food, cards, hugs, and good intentions. But I struggled to receive it.

Somewhere deep inside, I believed that accepting help meant I had failed. That I wasn't strong enough.
And you know what? I wasn't.
That hard truth finally cracked the illusion that I had to be. But here's the beauty:

Even in that place — even when I had no answers, even when I was angry and confused — God never left.

He didn't turn away when I asked Him hard, painful questions.
He didn't back off when I was frustrated or numb.
He didn't need a polished prayer or a perfect praise song.
He stayed.
Quietly. Faithfully. Always.

And over time, I began to see something I hadn't understood before: God wasn't waiting for me to fix everything or figure everything out. He was holding me closer in the questions than I had ever felt in the certainty. Let me put it another way: Sometimes we get lost — not because there's no way forward, but because we're too ashamed to admit we need help.

Picture someone on a long road trip. They miss a turn but keep driving, hoping things will work themselves out. The GPS quietly says, "Recalculating," but they turn down the volume. Not because they don't want help — but because they feel like they should've gotten it right already.

That's what keeps them stuck. That is what kept me stuck.
Not the wrong turn.
Not the detour.
The shame of helplessness.
And we do the same thing, don't we?

We resist grace because we think we haven't earned it. We push away help because we believe we should be past this by now.
We try to prove we're fine — when what we really need is the courage to admit we're still hurting.

But here's the truth I want you to hear:
God is not waiting for you to fix yourself.

He is already with you — in the detour, in the silence, in the confusion.

He's already speaking love over your pain. He's already offering peace, even when you don't know how to reach for it.

THE LIE OF ISOLATION

Have you ever been in a crowded room and still felt completely alone?

People are laughing, talking, brushing past you with plates of food and full lives—and yet you feel invisible.
Not because no one cares… but because no one sees what's happening inside you.

That's what emotional isolation feels like.
It's not about physical distance.
It's about the weight of carrying something no one else understands.

As an introvert, I've always needed alone time to recharge.
Solitude helps me think, breathe, and reconnect. But when I'm hurting, that instinct to be alone can quietly become a wall. The more I struggle, the stronger the urge is to withdraw—to smile and say, *"I'm fine,"* while my soul is quietly unraveling inside.

And sometimes, it's not just silence.
It's a silent scream.
Part of me is crying out, *"Help me, I'm hurting."*
But another part is whispering, *"Don't look too closely. Don't see too much."*
And pain, never missing a moment, slips in and hisses,
"You aren't normal. Everyone else is fine. Why aren't you?"

But here's what I've learned:
God sees through all of it—
The smile. The silence. The shutdown.

And He stays.
He doesn't flinch at the mess.
He doesn't turn away from the ache.
Even when I've pulled away from everyone else,
He's never pulled away from me and He won't pull away from you.

Pain often whispers lies like: *You're the only one.*
No one understands.
No one sees you.
If they knew your secret… (go ahead—fill in your worst fear.)

And if you've carried your struggle quietly, it's easy to believe those lies. To sit in silence because you're not sure anyone would understand the noise inside your soul.

But sometimes, it's not even the silence that's the hardest—

>It's the noise in your own head.
>>The racing thoughts.
>>The spirals of worry.
>>The questions with no answers.
>>The replay of what you said.
>>The regret of what you didn't do.
>>The things you wish you could forget.
>>The overthinking that never seems to sleep,
>>Even when your body is begging for rest.

But here's the truth:
You are not alone.

There are others walking through their own valleys, even if they never speak of it. Even if they look perfectly put together from the outside.

And more importantly—
God sees you. And He loves you.
He hasn't turned away.
He hasn't overlooked your suffering.
Even if you haven't felt His presence lately—**He has never once taken His eyes off you.**

Even there—
In the chaos of your thoughts—
God is present.
He's not intimidated by your overthinking.
He doesn't tune out your anxious heart.
He sits with you in the swirl.
And gently reminds you:
Peace is still possible.

"Where could I go from your Spirit?
Or where could I flee from your presence?
If I ascend up into heaven, you are there.
If I make my bed in Sheol, behold, you are there!
If I take the wings of the dawn,
and settle in the uttermost parts of the sea,
even there your hand will lead me,
and your right hand will hold me."
—Psalm 139:7–10 (WEB)

THE INVITATION OF GRACE

Grace doesn't kick down the door.

It doesn't arrive with fanfare or demand your best behavior.
Grace whispers. It waits. It reaches for you quietly in the middle of your mess.

Most of us have spent years trying to hold it all together. We've performed. We've pretended. We've powered through. And sometimes we've believed the lie that God only shows up when we've cleaned ourselves up first. But that's not grace.

Grace finds you in the worst of it—not the best of you.

It meets you in the hospital room, in the silence after the phone call, in the dark car ride home. It meets you when you can't find the right words to pray. It meets you when you're angry and confused and asking God *why*. It doesn't shrink back from your doubt. It doesn't flinch at your fear.
It says, "You are still loved. You are still mine."

That is the truth of grace: **it meets us in the middle of the mess.**

Grace doesn't ask you to clean up first. It doesn't wait for you to smile again or speak the "right" prayer.
Grace finds you in your lowest moment and says, "You are still loved. You are still mine."
Maybe you've heard the word grace before, but you're not sure what it really means. Let me tell you:

Grace is undeserved love.
It's the kind of love you don't have to earn.
It's being accepted when you feel unworthy.
It's forgiveness when you expected rejection.
Grace is God's heart reaching for you—not because you've got it all together, but because He loves you as you are.
You don't have to believe everything perfectly to begin this journey.
You just have to be open.
You just have to be willing to take one small step toward the One who's already walking toward you.
And that's what this book is—not a map out of the valley, but a companion through it.
A space to breathe.
A reminder that even here, even now, **healing is possible.**
You don't have to rush this.
There is no timeline for healing.
There is only today—and the gentle truth that God is with you in it.
So, take a breath.
Let your shoulders fall.
You made it here.
And that means something is already beginning.

"For by grace you have been saved through faith, and that not of yourselves; it is the gift of God."
—Ephesians 2:8 (WEB)

THIS IS JUST THE BEGINNING

You've made it through the first chapter—and that might feel like a small step, but it's actually a sacred one.
Because it means you've opened your heart, even just a little, to the possibility that healing is for you.
That grace isn't just a word—it's a hand already reaching toward you.

You don't have to have it all figured out.
    You don't have to feel strong today.
    But if you're here, reading this, it means you haven't given up.
    And friend—God hasn't given up on you either.

At the end of each chapter, you'll find a few gentle things waiting for you:

A short note called **"What I Hope You Know"**—a few truths I pray will settle into your heart. A personal prayer—because I am truly praying for you. And some reflection questions—to help you go deeper, honestly and at your own pace.

This is not a checklist. It's an invitation.
To pause. To reflect. To begin again.
Take your time. Be kind to yourself.

Let grace do what it does best—walk with you, one small step at a time.
You've already started.
And that means something is already beginning.

WHAT I HOPE YOU KNOW...

I hope you know that struggling doesn't mean you're failing.
    It means you're human.

It means you've been carrying something heavy, maybe for a long time.
And finally, you've reached the moment where you can stop pretending it doesn't hurt.
I hope you know that your breaking point doesn't scare God.
He doesn't back away from your pain.
He doesn't flinch at your honesty.
He moves closer.
I hope you know you don't have to keep it all together.
You're allowed to fall apart.
You're allowed to be tired.
You're allowed to not have the words.
And even if you've pulled away—God hasn't.
He still sees you.
He still hears you.
He still loves you.
God loves you. Right here. Right now. As you are.

MY PRAYER FOR YOU

Dear God,

For the one holding this book, for the one carrying more than they've said out loud,
Would You meet them right here?
In the weariness. In the questions. In the ache. In the silence.
Would You remind them that they are not forgotten?
That they are not disqualified?
That they are still worthy of love and still held by You?
When shame speaks loudly, speak louder.
When loneliness creeps in, remind them they are seen.
When they feel like they have nothing left, whisper the truth:
"You are mine. I'm not letting go."
Cover them in grace. Surround them with peace.
And walk with them—one step at a time—toward the other side.
Amen.

REFLECTION QUESTIONS

1. What are you carrying today? Please write it down without editing or judging yourself.

2. Have you ever felt like you were the only one struggling? What did that feel like?

3. When have you felt closest to God in the past? When have you felt furthest?

4. What would it look like to be honest with God about your pain?

5. Finish this sentence: *"God, right now I feel...*

CHAPTER 2
THE BREAKING POINT
THE MOMENT WHEN BROKEN FEELS BEYOND REPAIR

Sometimes, when I think about what it feels like to reach the breaking point, I think of watching surfers.

I've always been drawn to them—the balance, the timing, the sheer strength it takes just to stand up on a wave. It was something I could never do, no matter how many times I tried. But I loved to watch. There's something almost sacred about it—watching someone rise on a wave, knowing how many times they had been knocked down just to get there.

But what really stayed with me wasn't the ride.
It was the moment before.
The moment they were underneath it all.
Tumbled. Submerged.
Pulled under and held there by something bigger than they could control.

That's what the breaking point feels like.

You try to hold your breath.
You try to keep your bearings.
But everything is spinning.
You don't know which way is up.

And you wonder if you'll come back to the surface—or if you've gone too far under this time.

That's where some of us are right now.
Not riding the wave.
Not rising in victory.
Just trying to breathe at the bottom of something we didn't choose.
And if that's you, I want to say this as clearly as I can: **This is not the end.** Even at your lowest, **God sees you**.
Even beneath the wave, He is still holding you.

THE MYTH OF STRENGTH

Somewhere along the way, many of us were taught that being strong means never breaking down.
That to be faithful, or mature, or dependable, you have to hold it all together. That tears are a sign of weakness. That asking for help means you've failed. That falling apart disqualifies you.

But none of that is true.
It's a myth.
A lie.
A pressure we carry that **God never asked us to bear**.

The truth?

Being strong isn't about never falling—it's about knowing who to lean on when you do. And real strength? It's not always loud and polished. Sometimes, it looks like crawling out of bed in the morning. Sometimes, it's whispering a prayer when you don't even have the words. Sometimes, it's just staying—when everything in you wants to give up and disappear.

I used to believe I had to be the strong one. For my family. For my team. For my clients. For everyone.
I was a full-time caregiver for my mother in the late stages of her cancer, while also working full time in law enforcement.
There was no discussion about who would take care of her—it was simply understood.
I was the oldest. The daughter. And the expectation, both spoken and

unspoken, was clear. In many families—mine included—there's a deep, inherited sense of duty. Caregiving doesn't feel like a choice. It feels like a role you're born into.
And for daughters in particular, it often carries an invisible weight:

Be strong. Don't complain. Keep going. But behind the strength and the smiling and the "I've got this," I was unraveling.
I was emotionally threadbare.
I wasn't sleeping. I wasn't eating well.
And I was holding in a whole ocean of tears—because I thought letting them out meant I was weak.

But God didn't ask me to be superhuman.
He asked me to trust Him.
To let Him in—even when I didn't have the words.
To allow grace to catch me, not pressure to control me.

That's when I started to learn something important:
Maybe real strength isn't about holding it together.

Maybe it's about letting yourself fall—into grace.
Strength doesn't always look like standing tall.
Sometimes, it looks like finally surrendering.
Falling into rest. Into truth. Into God's arms.
But what happens when the collapse isn't visible?
When the world keeps spinning, but inside, something in you has completely come undone?
Let's talk about that kind of breaking point next.

THE QUIET COLLAPSE

Not all breaking points are loud.
Sometimes, they happen quietly—
At a kitchen sink.
In a parked car outside the grocery store.
In a bathroom stall at work, with the faucet running just loud enough to muffle the tears.
There's no dramatic scene. No big announcement.
Just the slow, steady realization that something inside you is unraveling—

and no one else knows.
The world expects you to keep moving.
To meet the deadline. To answer the text.
To fold the laundry.
And so, you do.
You function. You smile at the right times.
You say you're fine.
You even make jokes.
But inside?
You're exhausted.
Empty.
Barely hanging on.
That's the thing about pain—it doesn't always scream.
Sometimes, it just quietly chips away at your spirit until one day you realize... **you've been surviving, not living.**

I've had those seasons—the ones where I kept showing up for everything and everyone, while quietly falling apart behind the scenes. And the hardest part wasn't just the pain.

It was the silence.

The feeling that if no one saw it, maybe it didn't matter.
Maybe *I* didn't matter.
But here's the truth I want to gently offer you:
Even your quiet collapse matters to God.
Even when no one else sees it—He does.
Even when your voice is too tired to ask for help—**He's already drawing near.**

WHO ARE YOU NOW?

When everything falls apart, it doesn't just break your plans—it can shake your identity.

Who you were before the loss?
Before the poor decision?
Before the diagnosis?
Before the silence, the heartbreak, the unraveling?

. . .

Maybe you were the strong one.
>The dependable one.
>The one who got things done.
>The one people leaned on.
>The one who always made it work.
>But now… things have changed.

And whether it happened suddenly or slowly, you're standing in the aftermath wondering,

> **"Who am I now?"**

It's not just grief over what happened. It's grief over who you were before it happened. And that part—*the part no one else can see*—hurts differently. You might still be going through the motions. You're showing up. Smiling. Doing what's expected.

But inside, the questions are louder than ever.
You don't feel like yourself. And maybe you're afraid that you've lost something you can't get back.

But I want you to know this:

> **You are not lost.**
> You are not broken beyond recognition.
> You are not less than who you were before.
> Your identity hasn't been erased—it's being **refined** in this season.
> God hasn't forgotten who you are.

Even when you feel unrecognizable to yourself, **He still calls you by name.**

> *"Fear not, for I have redeemed you.*
> *I have called you by your name. You are mine."*
> —Isaiah 43:1 (WEB)

That's who you are.
    Not forgotten. Not forsaken.
    Still His. Always His.

YOU ARE NOT ALONE

There's a moment in every breaking season when we might quietly ask the question:
Where is God in all of this?

Not always in anger—though sometimes, yes—but often in confusion.
In grief. In profound soul exhaustion.

Because when everything falls apart, we start to wonder:
    If God is near, why does He feel so far?
    If He loves me, why does this hurt so much?
    But pain can cloud our vision.
    It doesn't mean God left.
    It just means we're human.
    It's hard to see clearly when you're in the storm.
    So, if you've asked that question, you're not wrong.
    You're not broken for wondering.
    You're not faithless for feeling far from Him.
    You're human.
    And still—**you are not alone.**

Even when the prayers are quiet.
Even when the questions outnumber the answers.
Even when your tears hit the pillow and it feels
like no one sees—**He sees.**
You are not alone in this.
Not because you've managed to be strong.
Not because you've handled everything perfectly.
But because **God is faithful.**
And He promised that even in your darkest valley, **He would never leave your side.**

He's not distant.
He's not waiting for you to be perfect.
He's right here—with you. Still near. Still faithful. Still holding on to you, even when you don't feel it.

> *"The Lord is near to those who have a broken heart,*
> *and saves those who have a crushed spirit."*
> —Psalm 34:18 (WEB)

If all you've got today is one more breath, one more step, one more whispered, *"Help me…"*

That's enough.

WHAT IF THIS IS THE BEGINNING?

When you're at your lowest, it's easy to believe this is the end of the story.

The end of your strength.
The end of your purpose.
The end of everything that once felt steady or sure.
But what if that's not true?
What if this breaking isn't your undoing—but your unfolding?

What if the pieces that feel scattered right now are actually being rearranged into something more whole than you've ever known?

God is a master at creating beauty from brokenness.

He doesn't rush you past the pain.
He doesn't demand that you understand it.
He simply sits with you in it—faithfully, patiently.
But He's not just sitting still.
He's working—even now.
Quietly shaping, restoring, redeeming.
You may not see it yet.
You may not feel it.

But there is still breath in your lungs.
And where there is breath, there is possibility.

> "See, I am doing a new thing!
> Now it springs up; do you not perceive it?
> I am making a way in the wilderness
> and streams in the wasteland."
> —Isaiah 43:19 (WEB)

You may feel like walking through a wilderness, but that doesn't mean you're lost. You may feel surrounded by ruins, but that doesn't mean nothing good can grow again.

And just because you can't see the other side yet doesn't mean it isn't already there. Because **that's the truth of grace—**

Grace meets you in the middle of the wreckage and reminds you:

> This isn't the end.
> God is still writing.
> The other side is real.

One of the most comforting things anyone has ever said to me came from my soul sister, Gloria. We've been doing life together for nearly forty years—and let me tell you, she is an angel on earth.

During one of the hardest seasons of my life, she looked at me and said gently,

"You survived 100% of your worst days."

That line hit me so deeply that I wrote it on a sticky note and put it on my computer. I needed to remember: I had made it through, and I would again.

If today feels like the end—
If everything feels too broken, too far gone, too painful to bear—
I want you to hear her words, too:
YOU survived 100% of your worst days.
You're still here.
And that means **God's not finished.**
This breaking point is real.
But it might not be your ending.
It might just be the beginning of the other side.

MY HOPE AND PRAYER FOR YOU

WHAT I HOPE YOU KNOW...

I hope you know that reaching a breaking point doesn't mean you've failed. It means you've been carrying something heavy—and you've reached your limit.

It's not weakness. It's human.

I hope you know that God doesn't back away when you're broken.

He moves *closer*.
He doesn't need you to hold it all together to be worthy of love. He's not shocked by your questions or ashamed of your tears. I hope you know that you're allowed to stop pretending. You're allowed to fall apart in the arms of a God who never will. You're allowed to admit that it's too much—and still be held by grace.

Your breaking point isn't the end of the story.

It might just be where the real healing begins.

———

MY PRAYER FOR YOU

Dear God,

For the one who feels like everything has come undone,
who's sitting in the middle of brokenness they didn't choose or didn't expect— wrap them in Your peace.

When they feel like they've lost who they are, remind them that You still see them. When they feel like they've gone too far under, be the breath in their lungs. When they're too tired to pray, hold their heart close and speak for them.

Thank You for never walking away.

For being the God who stays when everything else falls apart. For gently whispering, "You are still mine."
Let this be the beginning of something new.
Not in their strength—but in Yours.
Remind them: they are not alone. They are not forgotten.
And they are still held in love.

Amen.

REFLECTION QUESTIONS

1. When you think about your own breaking point, what stands out the most—what happened, or how it made you feel?

2. In what ways have you felt pressure to stay strong or hold everything together?

3. What would it look like to be honest with God about where you are right now—and trust that He won't walk away?

CHAPTER 3
THE GOD WHO NEVER LEFT
HIS PRESENCE IN SILENCE

Imagine a little child standing on stage for their very first school performance. The lights are bright—too bright. They squint, looking out into the sea of faces but can't see the one they're looking for. Their heart races. They freeze. And then, panic rises: *Where's my mom? Where's my dad?* The lights blur the view, and they can't hear the voices they know.

But what that child doesn't realize is that their parent is right there—in the crowd, in the shadows, fully present. Watching every move. Cheering with their whole heart.

They never left.

I think about that a lot when I remember the times, I felt like God had gone silent.

When I looked out into the mess of my life and couldn't *feel* Him there. But just like that child, I was never actually alone. I just couldn't see Him through the spotlight of pain.

As a parent, I understand this more than ever. There have been times I've stood in the background of my children's lives—cheering, praying, loving with everything I had—while they didn't even realize I was there. Not because I had abandoned them, but because I knew they needed to *learn, grow, struggle,* or *shine* in ways they could only do on their own.

I didn't walk away.

I just loved them from where they couldn't see me.

And now I believe God does the same.

WHEN GOD FEELS SILENT

One of the hardest things about suffering isn't always the pain itself—it's the silence.
    You pray, but the answers don't come.
    You read Scripture, but the words feel flat.
    You worship, but your heart feels far away.

You keep doing the "right" things… and still feel like you're walking through a fog where God seems just out of reach.

And to make it harder—you look around and see others being blessed.

       The healing. The engagement. The promotion. The peace.

They talk about God's goodness and blessings, and you smile (even if it is a fake one), but inside you whisper, *What about me?* Or wonder, *I volunteer more than she does.*

You start to wonder if you've done something wrong.
If you missed a check block in the, "How to be God's Favorite" checklist.
If God is blessing everyone else but has gone quiet on you.
And that quiet?
It's not just frustrating—it's heartbreaking.
Because when you're hurting, the one thing you want more than anything is *to feel close to God.*

And when He feels far away, it adds a layer of ache that no one else can see. But I want to speak this gently over your soul:

God's silence is not the same as God's absence.

He's not ignoring you.
He's not punishing you.
He's not standing off in the distance waiting for you to "get it right."

In fact, some of the most powerful moments in Scripture happened during what looked like silence.

Job sat in ashes, asking, "why".
David poured out pages of psalms that began with, *"Where are You?"*
And even Jesus cried out from the cross, *"My God, why have You forsaken me?"*

If you've ever asked those questions—if you're asking them now—you are not faithless. You are human. And you are loved. God doesn't shame you for not feeling close.

He stays close, even when your emotions don't recognize Him. And one day, you may look back and realize that even in the silence, **He never left.**

THE HIDDEN PRESENCE

Some of the most important things in life happen where no one can see them.

Roots grow deep underground before a single leaf appears.
A baby develops in the hidden safety of the womb, unseen for months.
Healing happens in the quiet—at the cellular level—before the surface ever looks different.
And faith?

Faith is often formed in the dark, long before it shines in the light.

God's presence doesn't always come with fireworks or goosebumps. Sometimes, it's so quiet we miss it.

Sometimes, it's working in ways we can't perceive until much later. But that doesn't make it any less real. God is not absent just because He's not obvious. He's not ignoring you just because He's not answering in the way you expected. Sometimes, He's doing His deepest work in the places no one else can reach.

If I'm honest, I'm always moving.
Always working, helping, doing.
Part of it is just who I am—but part of it, if I really think about it, is this:

When you stay busy, you don't have to sit with the pain.

You don't have to ask the hard questions or face the emotions waiting in the quiet.

When I finally stop and let the stillness settle in, I realize that God has been waiting for me there all along. If I am honest, sometimes the pain of whatever I am going through forces me to stop and to get still.

Jesus told us this plainly:
"But you, when you pray, enter into your inner room, and having shut your door, pray to your Father who is in secret; and your Father who sees in secret will reward you openly."
—Matthew 6:6 (WEB)

There is something sacred about the quiet.
  It's not about the location—it's about the posture.
  The slowing. The stilling.
  The whispering of a heart that dares to hope God is still near.
  He often doesn't shout.
  He whispers.
  And sometimes the only way to hear that whisper…is to slow down.
  To get quiet.
  To stop moving long enough to listen.

WHAT FAITH LOOKS LIKE IN THE DARK

Faith in the dark doesn't always look like singing worship songs with your hands raised or quoting the perfect Bible verse.

Sometimes it looks like crawling into bed and whispering, *"God, I hope You're still there."*
Sometimes it's not a roar—it's a whisper.
Sometimes it's not confidence—it's a question.
Sometimes faith isn't *loud* at all. It's just… **still showing up.** And that counts. **That matters.**

Faith doesn't have to feel strong to be real.
I used to think if I didn't feel close to God, it meant I wasn't doing something right.
But now I believe this:
Faith is choosing to reach—even when you don't feel anything reaching back.

It's holding on, not because the feelings are there, but because the *relationship* is. God never asked us for perfect faith.

He never said we had to get it all right.

In fact, Jesus said that even *mustard seed* faith could move mountains.
"If you have faith as a grain of mustard seed, you will tell this mountain, 'Move from here to there,' and it will move; and nothing will be impossible for you."
—Matthew 17:20 (WEB)

That means the tiniest flicker of belief in the darkness still matters to God.If you're showing up—even in silence, even in struggle—**you're doing more than enough.** God sees the fight inside you. He sees the quiet prayers. The brave steps. The way you haven't given up, even though you've wanted to. And He's not going anywhere.

HE STAYS

You might feel forgotten. But you're not.
    You might feel unseen. But He sees every tear.
    You might feel like you've drifted too far. But He's never moved.

"I will in no way leave you, neither will I in any way forsake you."
    —Hebrews 13:5 (WEB)

That promise is not based on how spiritual you feel or how steady your faith is.

> It's based on **who He is.**
> Unchanging.
> Steady.
> Faithful.
> Always near—even when your emotions can't catch up.

And beloved—He's there even when you're curled up on the cold bathroom floor, mid-ugly cry, wondering how you even ended up there.

> Mascara running.
> Tissues nowhere in reach.

The kind of moment where if someone walked in, you'd have to say, *"Don't look at me, just hand me chocolate."*

> Yes, **even there.**
> That's how steady His love is.

We serve a God who doesn't flinch at our fears or back away when we doubt.

> He stays.
> He stays when we're angry.
> He stays when we're numb.
> He stays when we cry and when we go silent.
> **He stays—because He's God, and because He loves you.**

LOOKING BACK TO FIND COMFORT

Sometimes the clearest proof of God's presence isn't found in the moment—it's seen in the rearview mirror.

You look back on a season that felt like silence…And suddenly you realize there were signs of His love all around.

The right person calling at the exact moment.
The doors that didn't open—because something better was coming.
The strength you had no idea you had.

It's not always obvious in the moment. But later—when the storm quiets, when the grief softens, when your heart has space to breathe—you begin to see it:

He was there.
    The whole time.
Not just in the healing, but in the heartbreak.
Not just in the recovery, but in the collapse.
Not just in the answered prayer, but in the ache of waiting.
He never left.

And looking back, you can trace His grace—not because the pain didn't happen, but because *you were never abandoned in it.*
Maybe you can't see it yet. That's okay.
But one day, you might look over your shoulder and see what you couldn't see before:

That even in the silence…
    Even in the struggle…
    Even in the moments that nearly broke you…
    You were never alone.

There's nothing that prepares you for the grief of losing someone you love—especially when life doesn't stop to let you grieve.

When my father had died suddenly, I had just become a CPA, and my dad had a small tax business that supported both him and my mom. She worked in the office too, but mostly handled the administrative side. I knew I had to sell the business quickly so my mom would have some financial security.
    There was just one problem:
    I had no idea how to sell a business.

I prayed. I had others praying for me. And then… I got this idea.
The phone book. Yes, the old-school kind with pages that leave ink on your fingers. I started calling every competitor I could find.
Page one. Page two. And then—by about page three—I found someone who was interested. Within 48 hours, they signed a purchase agreement.

A miracle, really.

But at the time, I was so deep in grief I couldn't see the full picture. I was just surviving—putting one foot in front of the other. Have you ever been in that situation?

It took years before I could look back and truly see what God had done.
    How He'd answered my prayer.
    How He'd made a way.
    How He'd held me—even when I couldn't feel it.

That's the thing about God's presence.
It's not always loud or instant.
Sometimes, it's only visible in the rearview mirror.
But once you see it, you realize it was there all along.

MY HOPE AND PRAYER FOR YOU

I HOPE YOU KNOW...

Sometimes the greatest comfort doesn't come from getting the answers it comes from realizing you were never alone in the questions.

You may not have felt God in the middle of the storm.
You may still be waiting to hear His voice or feel His presence.
But chapter by chapter, breath by breath, He has been with you.
Maybe not in the way you expected.
Maybe not in the moment you wanted.
But still—with you. Steady. Present. Unmoved.
And if all you can do today is look back and say, "I made it through,"—
that's holy too.

Because sometimes, survival is proof of grace.
Sometimes, hindsight is where the healing begins.
As we turn the page and begin to talk about what grace really is and how it meets us—right where we are—hold on to this truth:

You are seen.
    You are still held.
        And God has never left.

MY PRAYER FOR YOU

Dear God,

For the one reading these words—who may still feel unsure, unseen, or unsteady—would You wrap them in peace right now?

Would You whisper into their weariness, and remind them You've been there the whole time?

In every tear. In every silent prayer. In every breathless moment where they didn't know what to say.

Let them feel Your nearness in new ways.
Not because they've done anything special—but because You are always faithful.

God, thank You that You never change, even when we do.

Thank You that You love us—not for our strength, but in our surrender.
And thank You for never walking away.

Remind this precious soul:
Even if they can't see the way forward yet,
they're not walking it alone.

Amen.

REFLECTION QUESTIONS

1. Have there been moments in your life where you felt God was silent? Looking back, can you now see His presence in any way?

2. What emotions or beliefs come up for you when you feel disconnected from God?

3. What would it look like to create space for quiet in your life this week—just to be still and listen?

CHAPTER 4
TRUTH OF GRACE
GRACE MEETS YOU RIGHT WHERE YOU ARE

Grace is not a theory.

It's not a theological concept meant only for pastors or perfect people. It's not a reward you earn after getting everything right. **Grace is real.**

It's fierce, unearned, and personal.

It doesn't come with fine print or preconditions.

It finds you—right in the middle of your storm.

Because grace isn't the sunshine after the storm—it's the umbrella that finds you in the downpour. When you're soaked in regret, shame, or sorrow, grace doesn't stand at a distance shouting instructions. It doesn't say, *"Come back when you're dry."* It steps into the mess, holds the umbrella over your head, and walks you home.

Grace doesn't wait for the rain to stop.
It joins you in it.

"For by grace you have been saved through faith, and that not of yourselves; it is the gift of God."
—Ephesians 2:8 (WEB)

THE MISUNDERSTANDING OF GRACE

Somewhere along the way, many of us picked up the idea that grace is a reward. While I love a Holy Rewards app on my phone when we've prayed enough, behaved well enough, served enough, or kept our spiritual life neat and tidy, that is not how grace works.

We think grace is for the ones who have it all together—
    the ones who don't yell at their kids,
    the ones who never question God,
    the ones who always remember scriptures.

So, when we mess up—
    when we fall apart,
    when we're angry,
    when we feel like we're failing at faith—
    we assume we've disqualified ourselves.
    But that's not grace.
    That's performance. And grace isn't based on performance.

The truth of grace is this:
    You don't have to earn it.
    You don't have to deserve it.
    You don't have to be "better" to receive it.
    Grace was never for the perfect.
    It was made for the broken.

And friend—if you've ever felt like you were too messy, too far gone, too complicated, too tired, or too late…
Grace was made for you

    It doesn't kick you out when you're a mess.
    It leans in and says, *"I already knew. And I'm not going anywhere."*

THE MESSY MIDDLE

Grace doesn't wait at the edge of the mess, holding its nose and tapping its foot.

It steps into the middle of the chaos with you—unafraid, unshaken, and unwavering.

It doesn't ask you to clean up first.
It doesn't expect you to have answers or a timeline.
It doesn't roll its eyes at your tears or your doubt or your anger.
It just stays.

Because real grace doesn't come with a clipboard and a checklist. It comes with compassion. It knows healing is not linear, grief is not tidy, and faith isn't always loud.

> Maybe no one told you this, so I will:
> You can be healing and hurting at the same time.
> You can still be overwhelmed and deeply loved.
> You can be in the *middle* of the mess—and still be held by grace.

There's this idea that we have to "get through it" before God can use us. Before He'll draw near. Before we're allowed to speak or lead or dream again. But that's not the heart of God. He doesn't require polished stories.

He meets us in the raw, unedited chapters—the ones with frayed edges and unfinished sentences.

Grace is the love that sits beside you in your worst moment and whispers, *"I'm not going anywhere."*

A STORY OF GRACE

She walked into the church ten minutes late, mascara smudged and flaked - keys still in hand. Praying that she wasn't wearing any of her clothes inside out.
> You could tell it had taken everything just to show up.
> She didn't sit in her usual spot. She didn't have her Bible.

She didn't even make eye contact—just slid into the back row like she was hoping not to be seen.

> But someone saw her.
> Not to judge.
> Not to fix.
> Just to sit beside her.
> No words. Just presence.
> That's grace.
> Not a sermon.
> Not a solution.

Just someone choosing to stay when walking away would have been easier. That woman didn't walk away with all her problems fixed. But she walked out knowing something she hadn't known when she came in:

> **She wasn't too far gone.**
> **She wasn't alone.**
> **She was still deeply loved.**

That's the first crack in the wall.
> Sometimes, grace doesn't kick the door down.
> It just *opens it a little,* so light can start to pour in.

INVITATION TO REST

Maybe no one ever told you this before:
> You don't have to try so hard to earn what's already yours.
> You don't have to perform to be accepted.
> You don't have to prove your worth to be loved.
> You don't have to reach perfection to receive grace.

God never asked you to be perfect—He just asked you to come.

I don't know about you, but I feel like a deep sense of relief when I am around people that allow me to be imperfect and still love me anyways…no matter what.

Some of us have spent our whole lives trying to *deserve* something God already gave freely. We carry guilt like it's holy.
We wear shame like its armor.
We hustle for approval—even from a God who already called us His.

But grace says you can sit down now.
- You don't have to keep striving.
- You don't have to keep carrying it all.
Grace says, **"Let's take a moment to rest."**

"Come to me, all you who labor and are heavily burdened, and I will give you rest."
    —Matthew 11:28 (WEB)

So, take a breath, beloved.
> You're not behind. You're not broken.
> **You are exactly where God can meet you.**
> Not once you've cleaned everything up.
> Now. Right here. Just as you are.

MY HOPE AND PRAYER FOR YOU

WHAT I HOPE YOU KNOW...

Grace is not a reward for the strong.

It's not a gold star for good behavior. It's not reserved for people who never mess up.

Grace is for the one who's exhausted from trying.
For the one who questions if they're too much—or not enough. For the one who can't even find the words to pray.

Grace is for *you*.

It doesn't show up when you've fixed everything.
It meets you in the middle of your mess and whispers,
"You are already loved. You are already mine."

I hope you know that you don't have to wait another minute to rest in that truth.
Not when the tears stop.
Not when the pieces are back together.
Now. Today. Exactly as you are.

MY PRAYER FOR YOU

Thank You for being the kind of God who doesn't wait for us to have it all together.

Thank You for grace that reaches down into the mess and calls us by name.

For the one reading this—tired, unsure, or overwhelmed—remind them that they are already enough in Your eyes.

Wrap them in Your love today. Quiet the voice of shame.

Let them feel the steady truth of Your presence.

God, help them stop striving for what You've already given freely.

Give them the courage to rest.

The strength to trust.

And the peace that only grace can bring.

Thank You for never giving up on us—even when we give up on ourselves.

Amen.

REFLECTION QUESTIONS

1. Have you ever believed that you needed to be better or "do more" to receive God's love?

2. What does grace mean to you right now—in this season of your life?

3. What would it look like to stop striving and simply rest in the truth that you are already loved?

CHAPTER 5
THE LONG ROAD FORWARD
HEALING TAKES TIME

Healing doesn't happen all at once.
It's not a switch that flips.
It's not a straight line upward.
It's not a magic piece of chocolate.

It's more like a wound that closes slowly—layer by layer, not all at once.
Some days, it looks like progress.
You breathe a little deeper. You sleep a little better.
You laugh—and mean it.
And you think, *maybe I'm finally okay*.
But then something bumps that still-tender place.
A memory. A song. A scent. A holiday. A moment you didn't see coming.
And suddenly, what you thought had healed feels raw again.
It doesn't mean you're back at the beginning.
It doesn't mean you're broken.
It just means you're still healing.
And healing—real healing—takes time.

We live in a world that celebrates the comeback story.
But not always the quiet in-between. Not the long nights. The deep breaths. The ordinary days where the only victory is that you kept going.

This chapter is for *those days.*

The slow days.
The days when you're not sprinting ahead but simply putting one foot in front of the other—sometimes walking, sometimes crawling, sometimes just breathing.
And that is enough.
Healing doesn't move in straight lines. You think you're getting better, and then something—a smell, a memory, a date on the calendar—pulls you under again.
And in those moments, it's easy to think you're failing.
That you're doing something wrong because you're not moving faster.
But here's the truth: **healing is not a race.**

THE MYTH OF "QUICK FIX FAITH"

There's this quiet message that floats around in Christian circles—one that's rarely said out loud, but often felt:
If your faith is strong enough, you should feel better by now.
If you trust God, you shouldn't still be sad.
If you really believe, you should have already moved on.

Let me say it as clearly as I can:
That is not how healing works.
And it's not how God works, either.
Faith isn't a shortcut.
It's not a magic pill. It doesn't erase pain—it carries you through it.

The truth is, we want healing to happen fast because pain is uncomfortable. For us. For the people around us.

We want resolution. A clean ending. A testimony wrapped in a bow.
But real healing? It's holy and human and slow.
And it doesn't make you less faithful if you're still hurting.
It makes you *real.* And then there are the wounds that go even deeper.
The ones that don't have a neat timeline or an easy conversation around them.

The grief of losing someone to suicide.
The silence after a miscarriage.
The ache of a child lost to addiction.
The devastation of being the one left behind after violence—or the one who caused it.

These are the kinds of heartbreak that don't always fit into tidy testimonies.
They don't fade in a month. They don't get resolved with a Bible verse and a pat on the back.

And if you're carrying something like that—something others don't talk about, or don't know how to talk about—please hear me:
You are not forgotten.
You are not too broken.
And you are not alone.

God sees the pain you don't know how to put into words.
He doesn't look away.
And He will never rush your healing.

SLOW PROGRESS IS STILL PROGRESS

We live in a world that celebrates speed.
> Fast recoveries. Fast answers. Fast turnarounds.
> But real healing rarely moves fast. It moves faithfully.
> Some days, progress looks like getting out of bed.

Other days, it looks like taking a walk, calling a friend, or saying a prayer when it would be easier to shut down. And then there are days when the bravest thing you do is *just keep breathing and binge watch 7 seasons of a show.*

> That counts. All of it counts.
> Healing doesn't always feel like forward motion.
> Sometimes it feels like standing still.
> Sometimes it feels like going backward.

. . .

But just because you're not where you want to be doesn't mean you're not on your way. There's no gold star for healing fast. There's no finish line you have to reach by a certain time. The road is long, and winding, and uneven. But if you're still moving—still showing up, still reaching, still whispering *"God, help me"*—then you are not stuck.

You are healing.

Slowly. Quietly. And beautifully.

And if no one has told you this lately: **You're doing better than you think.**

Healing isn't just measured in milestones—it's measured in the moments you keep going, even when it would be easier to give up. Every tear. Every breath. Every prayer. Every choice to keep walking when you don't feel strong—God sees it all.
And He's not grading your pace.
He's walking beside you at the exact speed your heart can bear.

HOW GOD WALKS WITH US

If you've ever felt like God is disappointed in how long it's taking you to heal—please take a breath and let this truth sink in:

God is not rushing you.

He's not tapping His foot, waiting for you to get over it.

He's not annoyed that you're still crying.

He's not frustrated that you're still asking questions.

He's walking with you.

Not pushing.

Not pulling.

Just *present*.

Think of how a parent walks with a small child—matching their steps, slowing when they slow, stopping when they need to rest.

That's the heart of God.
He is not in a hurry to "fix" you.
He wants to walk with you.

. . .

He joins you on the messy, winding, uneven road that gets you there. Step by step. Tear by tear. Breath by breath.

"Even though I walk through the valley of the shadow of death, I will fear no evil; for you are with me."
—Psalm 23:4a (WEB)

Notice what it doesn't say:
It doesn't say, "You carried me over the valley."
It says, *"You are with me."*
Right there. In it. Beside me.
That's who He is.
That's how He walks.

I went through a season where someone in my family was battling addiction. It was hard to talk about—because on the outside, everything looked "fine." But I could feel it. I could see the signs, the disconnect, the damage. I tried to say the right things. I tried to make them see. But they weren't ready. And no matter how hard I tried; they just wouldn't listen. It hurt. I was afraid.

And the helplessness I felt as I watched them make choices, I couldn't control was overwhelming.
One night, I asked God, *"Why won't he hear me?"*
And I felt that gentle whisper in my spirit:
"Because it's not your voice that saves. It's Mine."

That was when I started to understand something:
Walking with someone doesn't always mean changing their path.

Sometimes it means praying behind the scenes.
Loving without fixing.
Staying close without pushing.
And that's how God walks with us.
Patiently. Tenderly.
Never giving up.
Always right beside us—no matter how long the road becomes.

. . .

He did get clean.

And not just for a little while—he's been sober for over 25 years now. Today, he helps others walk through their own recovery journeys.

That's the evidence of God's grace.

Not just that healing is possible—but that it can ripple outward and bring healing to others, too.

ENCOURAGEMENT FOR TODAY

Maybe you don't feel like you're making much progress.
Maybe you're tired of being in the middle—too far from where you were, but not quite where you want to be.
But here's what I want you to know:

You are doing better than you may think.

You are not behind. You are not broken.
    You are *becoming*.
    There is no shame in the slow road.
    No shame in needing time.
    No shame in healing day by day even if there is no progress.

God sees every tear, every breath, every choice to stay present when it would be easier to sht down.

He's not measuring your progress by the mile—He's walking with you at the pace your heart can handle.

    Some days you'll move forward.
    Some days you'll rest.
    And some days, you'll feel like you've taken a few steps back.
    But even then—you're not starting over.
    You're just being human.

And *God walks well with humans.*
Take the pressure off.
You don't have to sprint.
You don't have to impress anyone—not even God.
You just have to keep going.
And on the days when that feels like too much?
Just breathe. Just sit. Just be.
That's still part of the journey.

MY HOPE AND PRAYER FOR YOU

WHAT I HOPE YOU KNOW...

Healing isn't about getting over it. It's about walking through it—with grace in your steps and God beside you the entire way.

There is no shame in slow progress. No expiration date on healing. No such thing as "too long" when it comes to the heart. Even now—even here—you are still growing. And *you are still loved.*

A PERSONAL PRAYER FOR YOU

Dear God,

For the one reading this who feels like healing is taking forever—be their strength today. Remind them that they are held by grace, not performance.
Thank You for never rushing our healing, never shaming our pace, and never letting go when we're too tired to hold on.
Help this precious heart trust the journey—even when it doesn't make sense. Help them rest without guilt. Remind them that they are not alone.

    Amen.

REFLECTION QUESTIONS

1. What part of your healing journey have you been trying to rush or fix? How would it feel to give yourself more grace in that area?

2. When have you seen God walk patiently with you, even when you felt stuck or slow?

3. What does "progress" look like for you right now—not in someone else's story, but in your own?

CHAPTER 6
WHEN YOUR VIEW CHANGES
SHIFTING FROM PAIN-FOCUSED VISION TO HOPE-FOCUSED VISION.

There's a moment just before sunrise when everything is still gray.
You know the sun is coming—you trust that light is on its way—but in that moment, the world still looks like night. Nothing feels different yet. The shadows haven't moved. The cold hasn't lifted.

And if you didn't know better, you might think morning forgot to show up. But then—slowly, almost imperceptibly—the light begins to stretch across the horizon. It doesn't burst onto the scene with fanfare. It simply arrives.
Soft at first. Quiet. But steady.
And as the light increases, something shifts:
Not just around you, but *within you.*
Your posture relaxes. Your vision clears.

You see the same landscape differently—because now, you're seeing it in the light.

That's what healing does.
It doesn't always change your circumstances right away.
But it changes *you.*

And little by little, it helps you begin to see life—not just through the eyes of pain, but through the lens of **hope**.

HOW PAIN CHANGES WHAT WE SEE

Pain has a way of coloring everything.
    It blurs the good.
    It magnifies the hard.

It whispers lies in the dark: *You're alone. You're broken. It's always going to be this way.*

Even when we're surrounded by people who love us, pain can make us feel invisible. Even when God is near, pain can make Him feel far. Even when hope is on the horizon, pain can convince us it's out of reach. It doesn't mean we're weak. It just means we're human.

When we've been hurt, disappointed, or worn down by life, our vision shifts. We brace for more loss. We stop expecting good things. We question everything—even the things we once knew for sure. Slowly, without even realizing it, we start seeing the world not through the truth but through the lens of our pain.

It's like walking into a coffee shop wearing sunglasses.
At first, you don't even realize they're on. Everything looks dim. The room seems colder, duller. You might wonder why the lights are so low or the barista didn't smile. But the truth is—nothing about the room changed.
You couldn't see it clearly.

Pain is like that. It tints everything. It can make a warm space feel distant.
It can make people's kindness feel like pity.
It can make God's presence feel far away—even when He's right there.

You might be surrounded by good things—beauty, love, safety—and still feel numb. Not because they're missing, but because the pain has dimmed your view. But once you realize you've been seeing life through a tinted lens, **something begins to shift.**

Not all at once, and not always easily—but gradually, your eyes begin to adjust. And with God's help, you start to see the light again.

INVITING GOD TO HELP YOU SEE AGAIN

The first step to seeing differently isn't trying harder.
It's inviting God into the blur.
When your vision has been shaped by disappointment, betrayal, grief, or trauma, it's okay to admit that you don't know how to look for hope right now.

> It's okay to say, *"God, I don't see You in the midst of all of this—but I want to."*
> That simple prayer opens the door.
> You don't have to know what to look for.
> You don't have to manufacture joy or fake a positive attitude.
> You just have to *ask*.
> Ask Him to soften the parts of you that have gone numb.
> Ask Him to lift the heaviness that's clouding your view.

Ask Him to show you something that helps you remember that light still exists. And then wait. Not for fireworks or sudden clarity… but for the slow, quiet return of vision.

> *"Open my eyes, that I may see wondrous things out of your law."*
> —Psalm 119:18 (WEB)

That prayer—*open my eyes*—is one you can whisper on the hard days. On the bitter days. On the days when it feels easier to stay guarded, distracted, or discouraged. You don't have to pretend everything's okay. You just have to be willing to look again. Because God doesn't just give light—**He teaches us how to see it.**

MOMENTS WHERE GOD WAS CLOSER THAN YOU REALIZED

Sometimes we don't realize how close God was until much later.
We look back on a season that felt dark, heavy, or lonely, and suddenly,

in the remembering, we spot a moment. A detail. A conversation. A peace that didn't make sense.

Something that whispers, *He was there.*
>Not fixing everything.
>Not removing the pain.
>But quietly holding space for you in the middle of it.
>It might have been the friend who called at just the right time.
>The stranger who smiled at you when you felt invisible.

The moment you sat in silence, too broken to speak—yet somehow, you felt comforted.

>That was God.
>Not always loud.
>But always close.
>It's okay if you didn't see Him then.
>It's okay if you couldn't feel Him through the ache.

But now, as your heart softens and your vision shifts, you might notice Him in places you'd overlooked. You don't have to go digging through your past for proof. But don't be surprised if, one day, you find yourself thinking:
"I thought I was alone—but I wasn't."
Because **you weren't.**
You never were.

LEARNING TO SPOT THE GOOD—EVEN IN THE SMALL THINGS

When your heart has been through a long, hard season, it can feel safer to stay numb. Hope feels risky. Gratitude feels out of reach. And joy? Joy might seem like something for other people. But here's the truth:

>**Hope doesn't always come in grand gestures.**
>**Sometimes it shows up in the small things.**

A moment of quiet.
A deep breath that doesn't hurt.

A sunrise that reminds you that the darkness didn't win.
A verse that speaks louder than your doubts.
A laugh you didn't expect.
These small things matter.

They're not distractions from your healing—they're part of it. Gratitude changes how we see. It doesn't deny the hard—it simply refuses to let the hard be the only thing we see.

When we practice noticing the good, our lens shifts from *lack* to *abundance.* This reminds us that beauty is still worth holding on to even when life feels heavy.

It goes all the way back to the Garden. Adam and Eve had everything—peace, purpose, and a relationship with God—but the enemy didn't tempt Eve by highlighting all she had. He focused her attention on what she *wasn't* allowed to have.

That one tree.
That one boundary.

And in doing so, he distorted her vision. The same thing happens to us.

Pain, fear, and comparison can narrow our focus to what's missing.
But gratitude? Gratitude widens the view.
You don't have to force yourself to feel happy.
But you can begin to look for the fingerprints of grace in your everyday life. Noticing the good isn't pretending the pain is gone.
It just reminds your heart that pain isn't all gone.

Some days, rejoicing involves raising your hands in worship. Other days, it involves noticing that the sun is shining… and deciding not to hide from it.

> The good is still here.
> Even now.
> Even if it's small.
> And learning to see it again?
> That's a holy kind of healing.

YOU'RE NOT SEEING WRONG—YOU'RE SEEING DIFFERENTLY

When you've walked through something painful, your vision changes.
    It's not about pretending everything is fine.
    It's not about ignoring the hard parts of your story.
    It's about learning to hold both.
    Both the ache *and* the hope.
    Both the loss *and* the love.
    Both the pain that shaped you *and* the God who is still shaping you.
    That's not seeing wrong.
    That's seeing *differently*.

Healing doesn't mean you'll never have hard days again. It means your eyes know how to find the light, even when the shadows are still nearby.

It's okay if what you see now differs from what you used to believe.

It's okay if your view has shifted.
    It probably needed to.
    Because now, you're not just seeing through pain.
    You're seeing through grace.

MY HOPE AND PRAYER FOR YOU

WHAT I HOPE YOU KNOW...

You don't have to see everything clearly to believe that healing is happening. Even if it's still foggy. Even if your vision still trembles. **God is still at work.**

He's not asking you to have perfect clarity—He's just asking for a willing heart. And little by little, as you keep walking, reaching, and noticing, you'll start to see again.

A PERSONAL PRAYER FOR YOU

Dear God,

For the one whose vision has been clouded by pain, be the light that gently breaks through. When they can't see You, let them feel You. When they can't feel You, remind them that You never left.
Thank You for not rushing us toward clarity. Help this precious heart see the good again. Help them find You—even in the small, quiet things.

And may every glimpse of grace remind them:
They are healing.
They are seen.
They are loved.
Amen.

REFLECTION QUESTIONS

1. What are some things in your life that pain may have distorted your view of—yourself, God, others, or your future?

2. Have you ever had a moment where you realized God was closer than you thought? What helped you see that?

3. What's one small thing you can thank God for today—even if everything else still feels hard?

CHAPTER 7
PROGRESS IN THE MESS
WE ARE ALL A WORK IN PROGRESS.

I wasn't exactly what you'd call an outgoing kid. My friends and family see who I am now and are shocked by this confession.
Shy? That's an understatement.
Constantly filled with anxiety? Definitely.

At parties, I'd rather read a book than talk to strangers.

We moved a lot as a military family, and somewhere along the way, I decided it was easier not to make friends. Books didn't leave. Books didn't judge. So I stuck with books and writing my own stories.

Despite being shy and anxious, I wanted to fit in and be as "normal" as any high schooler could be. When I got to high school, my dad sat me down for one of those "life talks."

My shyness affected my grades because I did not participate in group projects or speak up in class. He said, "Everyone's afraid of something. But the people who push through fear—whether they succeed or fail—are the ones who can have anything they want."

Wait... *That's* the secret to getting anything I want?

After the hour-long "short lecture" and the obligatory teenage eye rolls, I went to my room, grabbed my journal, and started writing down my fears like a checklist.

At the top of the list? **"Make a friend."** I made a plan.

Instead of reading outside my classroom like usual at lunch, I'd walk around school and try to talk to someone. Day one: nothing. Day two: awkward eye contact. Day three: a few brave "hi"s to strangers who were probably more confused than welcoming.

Then on day four, I saw a girl reading a book outside a classroom, just like me. It was time to "make a friend"

Short blonde hair. Averting eyes. Same "I'm just surviving here" energy. With my heart pounding like I was about to deliver a TED Talk, I walked up and said: "Hi, I'm Janet. What's your name?" She looked up cautiously, like I'd interrupted her sacred reading moment. Decades later, we are still friends and laugh about my stalking and anxiety.

I still get nervous. I still overthink. I still have days when I want to hide. I still would rather curl up with a good book than to go to a party. But I've learned that showing up—shaky and unsure—is still showing up.

And every time I do, I feel God meet me there, saying, "Don't freak out."

That's the thing about healing and growth—**it doesn't usually come with a spotlight or applause.** It comes in small, unpolished moments that don't always feel brave at the time. Progress often looks like sweaty palms, racing hearts, and trembling first steps.
It's awkward. It's slow. It's vulnerable. And it absolutely counts.

BREAKING THE MYTH OF "HEALED MEANS FINISHED"

There's this idea floating around—sometimes subtle, sometimes loud—that once you've "healed," the pain should be gone.

No more sadness.
No more triggers.
No more messy emotions.

But that's not healing. That's *performing* wholeness. Real healing is quieter than that. It's not always visible. It doesn't always feel triumphant.

Sometimes healing looks like having a better day than yesterday.
Sometimes it's crying *and* laughing in the same moment.
Sometimes it's accepting trigger with a little more grace than before.

You don't wake up one day magically "over it."
You grow.
You shift.

You stretch into new space—sometimes awkwardly, sometimes unevenly—but it's still movement.

The truth is, **we reach the other side one small step at a time.**
It's not a leap. It's not a moment.

It's a slow, unfolding journey, and even when we think we've arrived, we may still carry reminders of the valley we passed through.

And you don't have to reach a perfect version of yourself to belong on the other side.

You're not just moving toward healing—healing is already happening. God is already meeting you in the middle of it.

The other side isn't a place for the polished—it's a place for the brave. And friend, you are braver than you think.

THE SETBACKS DON'T ERASE THE PROGRESS

Healing has curves, dips, and detours.

There are days when you feel strong… and then days when the same old fear, memory, or sadness sneaks back in and knocks the wind out of you.

And if you're not careful, it's easy to believe the lie: *I'm back where I started.*
>But you're not.
>You've grown.
>You've changed.
>You've learned how to breathe through the storm.

Even if the storm returns, **you're not the same person you were the first time it hit.**

A setback doesn't cancel the progress you've made. It doesn't erase the work God is doing in you. It's just part of being human—living in a world where healing takes time.

Even the disciples had doubts after the resurrection.
Even the heroes of faith had moments when they fell short.
And still, God never disqualified them.
He stayed close. He kept calling them forward.
And He does the same for you.

>That's the **truth of grace:**

It holds you when you stumble.
It steadies you when you slip. It doesn't require perfection—just a heart that's still willing to walk.
So, if you've had a hard day, a hard week, or even a hard year…It doesn't mean you've failed. It means you're still walking toward **the other side**—one sacred, imperfect step at a time.

HOW GOD MOVES IN THE MESS

We often assume that God moves when we've cleaned everything up—when we've figured things out, pulled ourselves together, and put the pieces back in place.

But that's not how God works.
    He moves right in the middle of the mess.
    In the unanswered questions.
    In the kitchen-floor breakdowns.
    In the hospital waiting rooms.
    In the "I don't know what to pray anymore" kind of days.
    God doesn't need a tidy heart to show up.
    He doesn't wait for your perfect surrender or your best version.

He meets you in the swirl—when emotions are tangled and thoughts are loud and nothing feels steady.

    That's who He is.
    He hovered over chaos at creation.
    He walked into storms and sat with the hurting.
    He reached for the outcasts and interrupted funerals.

Not because they had it together, but because **He always moves toward brokenness, not away from it.**

If you feel like your life is too messy, too loud, or too far gone—take a breath. He's already here. Not watching from a distance, but kneeling beside you.

    In the clutter.
    In the questions.
    In the quiet work of healing that no one else can see.

You don't have to sort it all out for God to begin His work. You just have to be willing to let Him in.

PERMISSION TO STILL BE HEALING

You don't have to be finished to be faithful.

You don't have to be over it to be moving forward.
And you definitely don't have to have all the answers to be held by the One who does.

Sometimes we put pressure on ourselves to be further along.

>To smile more.
>Cry less.
>Be stronger.

We worry that our ongoing struggle somehow disqualifies us from real faith, real joy, or real belonging. But healing doesn't come with a timeline. It's not a race. And it's not a sign of weakness if you're still working through it.

You're allowed to still be healing. You're allowed to have days that feel messy and moments that still ache. You're allowed to rest when you're tired and start again when you're ready. You're allowed to be a living, breathing, healing-in-progress human being.

>God isn't disappointed in you.
>He's not rushing you.
>He's not comparing your journey to anyone else's.
>He's walking with you, exactly as you are, one breath at a time.
>So let this be the reminder your soul might need today:

You don't have to be there yet.
You're still healing.
And that's okay.

MY HOPE AND PRAYER FOR YOU

WHAT I HOPE YOU KNOW...

I hope you know that healing isn't a one-time moment. It's a journey that unfolds—sometimes beautifully, sometimes painfully, often both at the same time.

I hope you know that your progress counts, even when it's quiet.
    Even when no one else sees it.
    Even when you feel like you're circling the same struggle again.

I hope you know that you're not failing because it still hurts sometimes. You're just healing. You're still becoming. And I hope you remember this:
    God is not waiting for the cleaned-up version of you.
    He's here. With you.

In the questions. In the chaos. In the courage it takes to keep going.
    You are not behind.
    You are not broken.
    You are healing—and He is with you no matter what side you are on.

A PERSONAL PRAYER FOR YOU

Dear God,

For the one who's still healing—still wrestling, still trying, still here — I ask for peace that quiets the pressure,and grace that silences the shame. Remind them that they don't have to be perfect to be progressing. That setbacks don't cancel the work You're doing in their heart. That even when healing is slow, it is still sacred.

Help them breathe today.
Help them rest without guilt.
Help them trust that they're not too far behind, too messy, or too late.

Thank You for walking with them through the fog, the tears, the questions. Thank You for being the God who stays in the middle—not just the God who waits at the end.

Hold this tender heart gently. Remind them:
They are not finished.
They are not forgotten.
They are still healing.
And they are still Yours.
Amen.

REFLECTION QUESTIONS

1. When have you felt like your healing "should" be further along? What has that pressure looked or sounded like?

2. What small signs of progress—no matter how quiet—can you recognize and celebrate in your life right now?

3. If you gave yourself full permission to still be healing, what would that change in how you show up today?

CHAPTER 8
FINDING YOURSELF AGAIN

Reclaiming identity after brokenness. Who you are in Christ, not in crisis.

Have you ever tried to force a puzzle piece into the wrong spot? It looks close enough—same colors, same shape, maybe just a tiny bit off. You press it, twist it, try from a different angle. It *almost* fits. And for a moment, you convince yourself that close enough is good enough.

But deep down, you know—it doesn't belong there.

And neither do you.

That's what it can feel like after you've walked through something painful or life-altering. You try to step back into who you were before. You try to fit into the life you had before the loss, the diagnosis, the heartbreak, the breakdown. But something's off. The shape of you has changed.

And here's the truth we rarely give ourselves permission to say: **You don't have to go back to who you were.**

. . .

You're not supposed to. Because you're not just picking up where you left off—you're becoming someone new.
    And that doesn't mean you're lost.
    It means you're still unfolding.
    You may not fully recognize yourself right now.
    You may feel out of place or unsure of where you belong.
    But your identity was never rooted in what you've been through.
    Your identity is rooted in who God says you are.

And He's never once been confused about you—even when you have.

WHAT CRISIS CAN STEAL FROM US

Crisis doesn't just hurt—it can *disorient* you. It shakes what you thought was steady. It blurs the line between what's happening *to* you and what's happening *in* you. And before you know it, you start to lose track of who you are. You begin to define yourself by the struggle.

The diagnosis.
    The divorce.
    The mistake.
    The title you lost.
    The label someone else gave you.
    The role you had to take on just to survive.

You may not say it out loud, but somewhere deep down, the narrative begins to shift:
    I'm the one who failed.
    I'm the one who got left.
    I'm the sick one. The broken one. The one who can't get it together.
    I'm too much.
    I'm not enough.
    That's what pain can do.

It tries to steal your name and replace it with something smaller. Something sadder. Something God never gave you.

    But hear this:

What happened *to* you is not the definition of who you *are*.
Your identity isn't your lowest moment.
Your name isn't your diagnosis.
Your worth isn't tied to your performance.
And you are not the sum of what fell apart.
You may feel like you're picking up the pieces.
But you're not just rebuilding—you're reclaiming.

YOU ARE NOT WHAT YOU'VE BEEN THROUGH

It's easy to confuse survival with identity.

When you've lived in crisis mode long enough, it shapes how you see yourself.

You get used to being the strong one. The fixer. The quiet one. The responsible one. Or maybe you've been called the dramatic one. The angry one. The difficult one.

Sometimes you even agree with it—when you're exhausted, grieving, or just trying to hold it together, those labels feel easier to wear than the truth.

What you've been through may have impacted you, but **it does not define you.**

You are not the mistake you made.
    You are not the trauma you carry.
    You are not the season that almost broke you.
    Yes, those things shaped you, but they did not finish you.
    God is still writing your story.
    And He's not using the labels the world gave you.
    He's calling you by name: **Loved. Chosen. Seen. Redeemed. His.**
The Creator of the Universe has called you.

. . .

You are more than your pain.
> More than your past.
> More than the things that tried to take you down.
> And slowly, gently, you're remembering that again.

WHO GOD SAYS YOU ARE

When everything around you changes—your roles, your relationships, your routines—it can be hard to remember who you are.

But that's when it becomes even more important to return to **who God says you are.**

> Not who people expect you to be.
> Not who pain convinced you to be.
> Not who your past tried to name you.
> Who *He* says you are.
> And He says…
> You are **loved** (Romans 8:38–39).
> You are **chosen** (1 Peter 2:9).
> You are **forgiven** (Ephesians 1:7).
> You are **God's masterpiece** (Ephesians 2:10).
> You are **redeemed** (Galatians 3:13).
> You are **held** (Isaiah 41:10).
> You are **never alone** (Deuteronomy 31:6).

That is the **TRUTH OF GRACE -**

That no matter what you've been through or how far you feel from who you used to be, *your identity has not changed in God's eyes.*

> You are still His.
> Still called.
> Still covered in love.
> The question isn't just "Who am I now?"
> It's *"Who have I been all along that pain tried to make me forget?"*

. . .

You may be in a season of rediscovery, but God never lost sight of you.
And He's gently, faithfully, calling you back to your name.

RECLAIMING THE PIECES

Rediscovery doesn't happen all at once.

You don't wake up one day fully restored, confident, and clear. It comes in moments.

> In glimpses.
> In pieces.
> And every piece matters.

Maybe it's the first time you laugh again and realize you missed that part of you. Maybe it's setting a boundary and realizing your voice still works. Maybe it's saying "no" when you always used to say "yes." Maybe it's picking up a long-lost hobby, calling an old friend, or simply resting without guilt.
> Those aren't small things.
> Those are sacred things.
> That's what reclaiming looks like.
> You don't have to go back to who you were before.

This is your invitation to become someone even deeper, more grounded, more whole, more real.

Piece by piece, God is helping you gather what's still true about you.

> Not just your strengths, but your softness.
> Not just your resilience, but your radiance.
> Not just the parts that survived, but the parts that are *ready to thrive.*

And it's okay if you don't have all the pieces yet. You don't need to rush. Because rediscovering who you are in this season? That's not a detour. That's part of the healing.

YOU'RE STILL BECOMING

There's a quiet kind of pressure that creeps in when you're trying to heal:
> *You should know who you are by now.*
> *You should be done with this already.*
> *You should be stronger, clearer, better… something.*

But what if you're not behind? What if you're just **becoming**? Becoming isn't about returning to who you were. It's about unfolding into who you're meant to be.

You're not unfinished because you're lost—you're unfinished because you're growing. Even when you don't feel it, even when your confidence wavers or your identity feels shaky—God sees what's taking shape inside of you.

> *"Being confident of this very thing, that he who began a good work in you will complete it until the day of Jesus Christ."*
> —Philippians 1:6 (WEB)

He's not rushing your transformation.
He's not disappointed that you're still in process.
He's patiently, lovingly shaping your heart and rebuilding your courage. Restoring what the world tried to take. And as you continue to walk through the healing, the questions, the quiet progress.

Just remember this:
> **You are not who you were.**
> **And you are not yet who you will be.**
> **You are becoming.**
> **And becoming is holy work.**

MY HOPE AND PRAYER FOR YOU

WHAT I HOPE YOU KNOW...

I hope you know that it's okay not to feel like yourself right now. Who you are is not defined by what you've lost or gone through or by who you used to be. It's not weakness to change—it's courage. And that healing doesn't erase your past—it simply refuses to let it hold your future.

I hope you know that becoming isn't about returning to who you were. It's about rising into who you've always been—underneath the fear, the roles, the heartbreak, and the noise.

God hasn't forgotten your name. He hasn't stopped calling you forward. Even now. Even here. You are still becoming.

A PERSONAL PRAYER FOR YOU

Dear God,

For the one who no longer recognizes their reflection, be their steady reminder.

For the one who feels unanchored or lost, be their gentle compass.

Thank You for never tying our identity to our performance, pain, or past.

Thank You for seeing us clearly—even when we can't see ourselves.

Help this beloved soul release the labels they were never meant to carry.

Help them reclaim what's still true.

Remind them that their worth is unshaken, their name is still known, and their future is still held.

Walk with them as they rediscover who they are—not by the world's definition, but by Yours.

> Piece by piece.
> Step by step.
> Wrapped in love.
>
> Amen.

REFLECTION QUESTIONS

1. What labels—spoken by others or yourself—have you carried that don't reflect who you truly are?

2. Can you name a piece of your identity you'd like to reclaim in this season? What made you feel most "you" in the past?

3. What does it mean to you to believe that "you're still becoming"? How might that bring freedom in your current journey?

CHAPTER 9
HOPE AHEAD
SPEAKING LIFE INTO WHAT'S NEXT.

After hours on the road, when your back is stiff and your heart is tired, you start to wonder if you will ever get there.

You've passed the same trees, fields, and stretch of highway so many times that it all starts to blur together. You've questioned your directions, your decisions, and your sense of timing. Maybe even your sense of self.

And then… you see it.
A sign.
Clear. Simple. Quiet.

It doesn't fix your exhaustion or shorten the road ahead, but it reminds you: *You're not lost. You're on your way.*

That's what hope can feel like—like a signpost for your soul.
It might not shout. It might not arrive with flashing lights or loud announcements. But when it shows up, even in the smallest way, it reminds you that forward is still possible.
Not because everything is fixed.
Not because you have all the answers.
But because something in you still dares to believe that there's more up ahead than what you've left behind.
That's the beginning of hope.

WHEN YOU DON'T FEEL READY FOR THE FUTURE

Sometimes, "moving forward" feels more like pressure than promise.

You've come through so much. You've worked hard to breathe again, to find solid ground beneath your feet. And now people are asking what's next… but what if you're not ready for what's next?
What if the idea of dreaming again feels scary?
What if hope feels fragile?
What if you're afraid of getting hurt again?
That hesitation is holy.
It means you're paying attention.

It means your heart has been tenderized by what you've walked through, and you're not rushing to build on shaky ground.

You don't have to leap into your future.
You don't have to fake confidence or force a smile.

Sometimes, hope begins with a whisper:
"Maybe… just maybe… there's more ahead for me."
And that's enough.

God doesn't demand blind optimism. He invites trust that acknowledges the wounds and dares to believe that He's not finished writing your story.

You don't have to be ready to run.
You have to be willing to take the next step, even if it's small.

LETTING GO OF THE OLD STORY

Sometimes the most challenging part of moving forward is not the unknown—it's releasing what used to define you.
You've lived through something that changed you.
You've carried pain, roles, expectations, or identities that were never meant to be permanent.
And even though they're heavy, they're familiar.

Sometimes it feels safer to stay wrapped in an old story than to risk writing a new one.

> But healing requires release.
> Not denial. Not erasing.

Just **letting go** of what no longer serves the future God is calling you into.

> Maybe it's the belief that you'll never be okay.
> Maybe it's the idea that you have to earn your worth.
> Maybe it's the pressure to go back to "the old you" when you know you've outgrown her deep down.

Letting go doesn't mean pretending it didn't matter. It means trusting **what's ahead is worth more than what's behind**. You can mourn the parts of your story you're leaving behind. You're also allowed to be excited about what comes next, even just a little.

> Because moving forward isn't a betrayal of who you've been.
> It's an act of honor.
> It's you saying, "I'm still here. And I believe there's more."

GOD'S PLANS ARE STILL IN MOTION

When life has fallen apart—or shifted in ways you never expected—it can feel like the plan is gone.
Like maybe you missed your chance.
Like maybe everything that once felt possible has been put on hold… or taken off the table altogether.

But here's what's true:
> **God doesn't abandon the plans He has for you.**
> Not because of loss.
> Not because of detours.
> Not even because of choices you wish you could undo.
> His plans may not look the way you imagined, but they are still unfolding. They are still holy. They are still alive.

• • •

"For I know the plans I have for you," says Yahweh, "plans to prosper you, and not to harm you; plans to give you hope and a future."
—Jeremiah 29:11 (WEB)

This verse isn't a shallow platitude—it was spoken to people in exile. People who had lost everything. People who weren't sure what their next chapter looked like.

Sound familiar?
God wasn't saying, "Everything's fine."
He was saying, *"I'm still with you. I still see what's next."*
Even if you feel like your timeline has been interrupted...
Even if you feel behind...
Even if you're still healing...
God's purpose hasn't expired.
And the story isn't over.

DARING TO DREAM AGAIN

There's a particular kind of courage required to hope again.
Especially when you've been disappointed.
Especially when the last time you dreamed, it didn't turn out.

It can feel safer to stay guarded. To keep your expectations low. To protect your heart from getting broken again.

But healing invites more than survival.
It invites you to *live* fully, freely, and faithfully. And sometimes, that means daring to dream again. Not with pressure. Not with performance. But with **permission.**

Permission to imagine what life could look like with joy. Permission to believe that laughter can return. Permission to pursue things that bring peace. Permission to build something new—even if it looks different from what you imagined.

Dreams don't have to be big to be meaningful.

. . .

They have to be honest.
    Maybe it's reconnecting with a piece of yourself you lost.
    Maybe it's trying something new.
    Maybe it's simply saying, "I'm open."
    Sometimes, hope doesn't start with a five-year plan in a black binder—it begins with a soft "yes" without knowing what will happen.
    And the moment you whisper it, the story shifts.

CHOOSING HOPE AS AN ACT OF FAITH

Hope isn't wishful thinking.
    It's not denial.
    It's not ignoring the pain or pretending the past didn't happen.

Hope is an act of faith.
It says, *"I believe God is still good, even when life doesn't make sense."*
It whispers, *"There's more ahead, even when I can't see it yet."*
Choosing hope isn't always easy.
In fact, it can be one of the most courageous things you do.
Because it means letting your heart believe again.

It means trusting that God is working even in the unseen.
It means looking forward—not because the road is clear, but because the One who walks with you is faithful.
You don't need all the answers to choose hope.
You need to take the next step in trust.
One small act of openness.
One honest prayer.
One breath of belief that maybe what comes next could be beautiful.

    That kind of hope?
    That's holy.
    And that's where everything begins again.

MY HOPE AND PRAYER FOR YOU

WHAT I HOPE YOU KNOW...

I hope you know that hope doesn't require perfection—it just requires permission.

    Permission to believe that healing is happening.
    Permission to take one more step, even if your heart is still afraid.
    Permission to let go of what was, so you can receive what's next.

I hope you know that you don't have to have it all figured out.

    You don't have to see the whole road ahead.
    You just have to trust the One who walks it with you.
    You are not stuck.
    You are not forgotten.
    You are still moving forward—even if it's slower than you'd like.
    There is **hope ahead**.
    And you are not walking toward it alone.

A PERSONAL PRAYER FOR YOU

Dear God,

For the one who feels unsure of tomorrow, would You be their steady place to stand? For the one who wants to hope but is afraid to try again—gently open their heart to possibility.

Remind them that hope isn't about ignoring the past—it's about trusting You with the future.

Thank You for being the God of new beginnings, quiet nudges, and unexpected beauty. Thank You for never rushing us forward, but always calling us forward.

When they are hesitant, give them grace.
When they are afraid, give them peace.
And when they begin to believe again—when they dare to dream or whisper a soft yes—

Meet them there with open arms.
Let this next chapter be one where they walk lighter, trust deeper, and believe again…even if it starts with just one step.
Amen.

REFLECTION QUESTIONS

1. What fears or hesitations do you feel when you think about moving forward into something new?

2. Is there an old belief or story you're ready to release so you can begin imagining something different?

3. What is one small way you could begin to open your heart to hope again this week?

CHAPTER 10
KEEP MOVING FORWARD
THIS ISN'T THE END. IT'S A BEGINNING.

Imagine you've been sewing a quilt for years.

Some patches are bright—stitched during joyful seasons, prayers answered, moments you never want to forget. Others are darker, tattered, sewn with shaking hands during unbearable nights. Some pieces don't quite line up. Some are stitched through tears. A few patches are there to hold things together.

There were times you thought about putting it away altogether.

Times when you told yourself it wasn't worth finishing.

Times when you didn't know what you were making—only that you were trying.

But every so often, you returned to it.

Piece by piece.
Thread by thread.
And now, as you pause and look back, you realize something sacred:
It's not finished—but it's becoming something.
It's not perfect. But it's real.
It's full of grace.
And most importantly—it's yours.
Healing is like that quilt.
It doesn't have to be complete to be beautiful.
It doesn't have to look like anyone else's to matter.

And just because the stitching still continues doesn't mean you're not already living in something holy.

So now, at the close of this book, let me gently remind you:
This isn't the end. It's just a pause in your story.

> You're still stitching.
> You're still healing.
> And most of all—
> You're still moving forward.

THE JOURNEY HAS CHANGED YOU

Take a moment.
> Look back—not to dwell, but to recognize.
> You've walked through something real.

Maybe you crawled. Maybe you stumbled. Perhaps you cried ugly tears through most of it.
But you didn't give up.

There was a time you weren't sure you'd make it this far.
And now… here you are.

> Still breathing.
> Still believing—at least enough to keep going.
> Still becoming someone deeper, softer, wiser than you were before.
> And maybe no one else noticed the progress.
> Maybe it didn't look dramatic or brave on the outside.
> But *you* know.
> You know what it cost to keep showing up.
> You know what it took to choose grace when shame felt easier.
> You know how hard it was to trust that healing could even begin.
> Let's say it clearly:
> **The journey has changed you.**

Not in a way that broke you, but in a way that rebuilt something inside of you.
> Your strength looks different now.
> Your softness has more depth.
> Your compassion has more weight.

You've become the kind of person who can sit with pain—and also reach for hope.

> That's no small thing.
> That's sacred growth.

YOU'RE NOT WHO YOU WERE, AND THAT'S A GOOD THING

There's something bittersweet about realizing you've changed.
> Maybe you don't laugh as quickly.
> Maybe you think more deeply.
> Maybe you're slower to trust, but quicker to notice what matters.

There are parts of you that feel unfamiliar now—not worse, just different.
And that can feel unsettling.
You might even grieve the version of you who existed *before*.

> Before the loss.
> Before the diagnosis.
> Before the betrayal, the burnout, the breaking point.
> But let me tell you something important:

That version of you wasn't wrong… it was just earlier in the story.

And you? You're still here—still writing, still growing, still becoming.

> You're not who you were.
> But you're not supposed to be.

You've also gained resilience, clarity, courage, discernment, and compassion.

You've learned to sit in silence without losing yourself.

You've discovered that you don't have to have all the answers to take the next step. And most importantly, you've learned that **you are more than what happened to you.**

You are a soul in progress—refined by pain, held by grace, and still deeply, unshakably loved by God.

> Don't be afraid of the change.
> Honor it.
> Let it tell the truth about how far you've come.
> Let it point to what's still possible.
> You're not who you were.
> And that's a good thing.

GOD WALKS WITH YOU INTO WHAT'S NEXT

There's comfort in knowing you're not walking alone.
> But it's more than comfort—it's truth.
> God didn't just meet you in the struggle.

He's not only the God of the breaking point, or the valley, or the healing

He is also the God of what comes next.
He goes before you.
He walks beside you.
He hems you in—behind and before.
And even when you're unsure of the path ahead, He already knows the way.

"Yahweh himself is who goes before you. He will be with you. He will not fail you nor forsake you. Don't be afraid. Don't be discouraged."
—Deuteronomy 31:8 (WEB)

He's not waiting for you to figure everything out. He's not standing at some finish line with His arms crossed, expecting perfection.

> He's in every small step you take.
> He's in the detours. The pauses. The deep breaths.

He's in the "I'm not sure I can do this" moments—and the moments you do.

> You don't have to have it all mapped out.
> You have to remember this: **He's walking with you.**
> Into the new.
> Into the unknown.
> Into the other side.
> And His presence will carry you—again and again.

A CALL TO KEEP GOING

This book was never about quick fixes.

It was never about tying a bow around your pain or pretending things didn't hurt.

It was always about *walking with you*—step by step, breath by breath—toward something deeper.

> Toward wholeness.
> Toward truth.
> Toward the kind of healing that doesn't just mend, but transforms.
> And that journey? It's still unfolding.
> So here's the invitation:
> **Keep going.**
> Even if your steps are small.
> Even if your faith feels fragile.
> Even if, on some days, "progress" looks like getting out of bed and whispering a single prayer.

Keep showing up to your life—not because you're unbreakable, but because you're brave. Keep honoring your healing—not because it's linear, but because it's *sacred*.

You don't need to have it all together.
You don't need a picture-perfect finish line.

What you need is already within you, planted and nourished by the **truth of grace**.

And that grace says:
You are not behind.
You are not disqualified.
You are not too far gone.
You are becoming.
You are healing.
You are loved—right now, not later.

So don't stop now.
Not when you've come this far.
Not when God is still walking beside you.
This life you're rebuilding?
This faith you're reclaiming?
This voice you're learning to trust again?
It's not the end of your story.
It's the continuation of something beautiful.

Take a breath.

Take one more step. And let the truth of grace carry you forward—into whatever God is preparing next.

THE OTHER SIDE IS ALREADY WITHIN REACH

Maybe when you first started reading this book, you couldn't see it.

Maybe you were still standing in the rubble—numb, unsure, exhausted.
Maybe you were in survival mode, just trying to make it through the next hour, the next conversation, the next wave of pain.
And yet, here you are.
Not because it's all fixed.
Not because you've reached some final destination.

But because you've kept moving.
You've kept breathing.
You've kept believing—just enough—to keep going.
And that? That's how you reach **the other side**.

Not in one dramatic leap, but through every small, grace-filled step you've already taken. The other side isn't just about a healed heart or a perfect ending.

It's about seeing differently.
Living differently.

Loving yourself and God and others from a place of wholeness—even if some of the pieces still don't make sense. It's about realizing that God wasn't waiting for you on the other side. **He was walking with you the entire time.**

And now you get to look up—not just with survival in your bones, but with hope in your spirit.
You've crossed through hard things.
You've carried heavy burdens.
But grace has carried you too.
And now?
The light is breaking through.
The weight is lifting.
The story is still being written.
You're standing at the edge of what's next.
And the other side is no longer just a promise—it's your present.

MY HOPE AND PRAYER FOR YOU

WHAT I HOPE YOU KNOW.

I hope you know this isn't the end—it's a continuation.

A sacred pause in your journey. A quiet turning of the page.

I hope you know that healing was never about returning to who you were… It was about becoming who you were always meant to be.

I hope you know that your story matters.

Not just the highlight reel, but the broken pieces, the unanswered prayers, the quiet victories.

And I hope you remember this:

You are never walking alone.

Not in the grief.

Not in the questions.

Not in the long, slow process of becoming.

God is still with you.

Grace is still holding you.

And the other side isn't a far-off destination—it's the life you're stepping into right now.

Keep moving forward.

You're closer than you think.

A PERSONAL PRAYER FOR YOU

Dear God,

For the one who turned these pages with a trembling heart and an open soul—thank You.

> Thank You for meeting them here. Thank You for never letting go.
> May they walk forward not with pressure, but with peace.
> Not with perfection, but with presence.

Let them feel Your nearness—not just in the high moments, but in the ordinary, everyday grace.

Remind them that healing is holy, even when it's slow.
> That progress still counts, even when it's quiet.
> That their journey is not forgotten, and neither are they.
> When doubt creeps in, whisper truth.
> When shame tries to rise, speak love.

And when they feel like they can't take another step, carry them—like You always have.

> Let them move forward with courage.
> With gentleness. With hope.
> Amen.

REFLECTION QUESTIONS

1. What are some ways you've grown or changed during this journey that you want to carry forward with you?

2. When you think of "the other side," what does that look like for you? How can you begin to live from that place—even in small ways—today?

3. What would it look like to fully trust that God is walking with you into whatever comes next?

CHAPTER 11
INVITATION TO FAITH

Beloved,
   I am praying for you.
   Maybe you read this book without knowing exactly where you stand in faith. Maybe it's been a long time since you even thought about it. Or maybe you've been so deep in grief, shame, or heartbreak that the idea of *the other side* felt like a fairy tale—something meant for everyone but you. And if you're not sure about God right now, I want you to hear this clearly:
   That's okay.
   You don't have to come with all the answers.
   You don't have to have it all figured out.
   This is not about religion, performance, or perfection.

This is an invitation to a relationship built on grace, not pressure.

God isn't waiting for you to clean yourself up or get it all right before He welcomes you.

   He's already been reaching for you, even if you haven't realized it.
   Even now, He sees you.
   He loves you.
   And He's inviting you home.

If You're Ready to Say Yes…

There's no magic formula—only a sincere heart. If you want to begin a relationship with God, you can pray something like this:

God,

I don't have all the answers, but I want to know You.

I believe You love me.

I believe You sent Jesus to bring me back to You.

I'm tired of doing this alone.

I'm ready to surrender the pain, the questions, and the pieces of my life to You.

I receive Your grace.

I ask for Your forgiveness.

I open my heart to Your healing.

Lead me from this day forward.

I want to walk with You to the other side.

Amen.

www.ingramcontent.com/pod-product-compliance
Lightning Source LLC
Chambersburg PA
CBHW072026060426
42449CB00035B/2704